Mega Military Machines™
Megamáquinas militares™

SHIPS

BARCOS

Catherine Ellis

Traducción al español: María Cristina Brusca

PowerKiDS press. & **Editorial Buenas Letras**™

New York

Published in 2007 by The Rosen Publishing Group, Inc.
29 East 21st Street, New York, NY 10010

First Edition

Editor: Amelie von Zumbusch
Book Design: Greg Tucker
Layout Design: Lissette González

Photo Credits: Cover image by Journalist 2nd Class Sarah Bibbs, U.S. Navy; p. 5 by Mass Communication Specialist 1st Class Robert J. Fluegel, U.S. Navy; pp. 7, 15, 23 Shutterstock.com; p. 9 by Mass Communication Specialist 1st Class James E. Foehl, U.S. Navy; p. 11 © Koichi Kamoshida/Getty Images; p. 13 © Pepe Diaz/AFP/Getty Images; p. 17 © Marcel Mochet/AFP/Getty Images; p. 19 by Mass Communication Specialist 3rd Class Roland Franklin, U.S. Navy; p. 21 © Michael D. Kennedy/U.S. Navy via Getty Images.

Cataloging Data

Ellis, Catherine.
    Ships / Catherine Ellis; traducción al español: María Cristina Brusca. — 1st ed.
        p. cm. — (Mega military machines–Megamáquinas militares)
    Includes index.
    ISBN-13: 978-1-4042-7623-9 (library binding)
    ISBN-10: 1-4042-7623-8 (library binding)
    1.Ships—Juvenile literature. 2. Spanish language materials I. Title. II. Series.

Manufactured in the United States of America

Contents

Contenido

Military ships are strong ships that were built to fight. Many military ships are part of the navy.

Los barcos militares son fuertes y están construídos para pelear. Muchos barcos militares pertenecen a la marina de guerra.

The front end of a ship is called the bow. The back end is called the stern.

El frente de un barco se llama proa. La parte trasera se llama popa.

The people who work on a ship are called sailors.

A las personas que trabajan en los barcos se les llama marinos.

The **captain** is the leader of all the sailors on a ship.

El **capitán** es el líder de todos los marinos de un barco.

There are many kinds of military ships. They all work together to fight wars.

Hay muchas clases de barcos militares. Los barcos militares trabajan juntos para pelear en las guerras.

This ship is a **destroyer**. Destroyers are fast. Some destroyers can go faster than 35 miles per hour (56 km/h).

Este barco es un **destructor**. Los destructores son muy rápidos. Algunos pueden navegar a más de 35 millas por hora (56 km/h).

This ship is an aircraft carrier.
Aircraft carriers are the
biggest kind of military ship.

Este barco es un portaviones.
Los portaviones son los
barcos militares más grandes.

Planes can take off from aircraft carriers. Planes can land on aircraft carriers, too.

En los portaviones, los aviones pueden despegar y aterrizar.

This boat is a hovercraft.
It can go on both land
and water.

Esta nave es un hovercraft.
Puede andar por el agua y
la tierra.

This is a **coast guard** boat. The coast guard keeps the shores safe and helps lost sailors.

Este es un barco guardacostas. Los barcos de la **guarda costera** protegen las costas de un país y ayudan a los marinos perdidos.

captain (KAP-tun) The leader of a ship.

coast guard (KOHST GARD) The part of the military that patrols the waters.

destroyer (dih-STROY-ur) A fast military ship with many arms.

---

capitán (el) El líder de un barco.

destructor (el) Un barco militar muy rápido que tiene muchas armas.

guarda costera (la) Grupo militar que patrulla las aguas.